Isadora Duncan

ISADORA Duncan

a graphic biography

WRITTEN AND ILLUSTRATED BY

SABRINA JONES

Paul Buhle, Editor

A NOVEL GRAPHIC from HILL AND WANG

A division of FARRAR, STRAUS AND GIROUX • NEW YORK

Hill and Wang
A division of Farrar, Straus and Giroux
18 West 18th Street, New York 10011

Library of Congress Cataloging-in-Publication Data
Jones, Sabrina, 1960–
    Isadora Duncan : a graphic biography / written and illustrated by
Sabrina Jones ; Paul Buhle, editor.
        p. cm
    Includes bibliographical references.
    ISBN-13: 978-0-8090-9497-4 (hardcover : alk. paper)
    ISBN-10: 0-8090-9497-5 (hardcover : alk. paper)
        1. Duncan, Isadora, 1877–1927. 2. Dancers—United States—
Biography. I. Buhle, Paul, 1944– II. Title.

    GV1785.D8 J66 2008
    792.802'8092—dc22
    [B]

                                                2008017928

www.fsgbooks.com

1 3 5 7 9 10 8 6 4 2

TO STEVE STERN,

who has an eye for dance, an ear for language,

and a good influence on me

CONTENTS

Foreword	*ix*
Introducing Isadora	3
The California Faun	9
Dancing Cross-Country	12
New York	14
London	17
Paris	21
Enter Romeo	25
Modern Odyssey	31
Germany Adored Isadora	36
Slave of Aphrodite	39
Barefoot in St. Petersburg	42
Snowdrop in the Dunes	47
Postpartum	50
Back in the USA	54
My Millionaire	58
Orpheus	62
Going Under	64
The Temple of the Dance of the Future	69
NY	74
Revolt of the Isadorables	80
A New World	87
Sergei Esenin	96
Honeymoon Roadshow	99
Emergency Exit	110
Flotsam	112
Adieu	118
After Isadora	123
Selected Bibliography	*127*
Acknowledgments	*129*

FOREWORD

by Lori Belilove

The first time I ever heard of Isadora Duncan I was thirteen. When
traveling with my family in Greece, I met an extraordinary Greek
dancer. He had a lock of Isadora's hair in a frame with her picture.
Singling me out as an heir to Isadora's legacy, he set me on the path
that would become my life's work. Who was this mythic figure, called
the mother of modern dance and the muse of modernism? She
was a California girl, like myself, who revolutionized the art of dance
at the turn of the last century. Back in Berkeley, I immediately read
Isadora's autobiography, *My Life*, and, at the moment of that reading,
I was triggered to find out everything I could about her and her dance.
This set me on an artistic pilgrimage, researching the last remaining
Duncan dancers and scholars. I traveled from Santa Barbara to New
York, to London, and then to Paris, Italy, and Germany. What I found is
that Isadora's dances and technique have been handed down through
generations of Duncan dancers who trained and studied with her and
her sister, Elizabeth, in schools she founded in Germany, France,
America, and Russia.

Isadora's sensational personal life has been the subject of movies,
plays, and more than forty books of varying accuracy, from the
scholarly to the simplistic. Her artistic contribution is often lost in
the fray. The free lover, the tragic mother, the glamorous expatriate,
the zealous revolutionary, and her freak accidental death can easily
overshadow the disciplined dancer, the choreographer, and the
founder of schools.

When I was sixteen, I returned to Greece to study Duncan dance
with Vassos Kanellos, the man who first told me about Isadora. Later,
I studied with two of her star pupils and adopted daughters, Anna
and Irma Duncan, and then with Hortense Kooluris and Julia Levien,
among many others. Eventually, after years of training, performing,

and teaching the repertory, I founded the Isadora Duncan Dance Foundation and Company to preserve her vast repertory of dances and technique. Based in New York City, the company is dedicated to not only performing and teaching her dances, but to the creation of new choreographies. The work lives on today for all seekers of truth and beauty.

Sabrina Jones has created a wonderful entrée into the life and art of Isadora. Don't let the comic format fool you: this playful work is accurate and serious. It captures the essence of Isadora's wild and determined personality. The story moves swiftly, but all the important details are there, covering the bold choices she made as well as the tragic destiny over which she had no control. I have selected many of the same anecdotes for my dance theater productions on the life and art of Isadora. Just as I use these stories to engage jaded high-school students and skeptical college undergrads, the book uses the drama of Isadora's life to forge an understanding of her art, why it shocked some and inspired others. The drawings make the ideas more accessible to younger readers, but they also enrich the story for readers of all ages, giving a visual sense of the era, Isadora's emotions, and the dynamic range of her dance movements.

Isadora Duncan became an international celebrity, a household name, and an icon of freedom. But she has always been regarded less seriously in her native America than in Europe, where she lived and worked for most of her adult life. She believed the remnants of puritanism kept Americans from seeing the lofty ideals behind her outré behavior and risqué costumes, and she certainly delighted in provoking them.

This book is an invitation to discover a great American artist, now that we are no longer outraged or titillated, to appreciate her audacity, her vulnerability, and her breakthrough achievements.

ISADORA DUNCAN

FIRST, THERE'S ISADORA'S VERSION — FULL OF BRAVADO.

What guts!

MY LIFE
ISADORA DUNCAN

PAY MY WAY TO EUROPE, AND YOU'LL BE HAILED FOR RECOGNIZING AN IMPORTANT AMERICAN TALENT.

OH, ROMEO, MARRIAGE IS ABSURD AND ENSLAVING! ESPECIALLY FOR ARTISTS.

SHE DANCED FOR THE RICH...

EXPENSIVE TICKET

... TO GIVE TO THE POOR.

FREE SCHOOL

BUT IF YOU READ HER ALONGSIDE OTHER SOURCES...

You go, girl!

MY LIFE
ISADORA DUNCAN

SHE LIED!

A BIO-graphy

11

THE DUNCANS SUBLET THEIR CARNEGIE HALL STUDIO BY THE HOUR TO MUSIC TEACHERS.

BRRR! CAN WE GO HOME YET?

MOTHER, PLAY "NARCISSUS" BY NEVIN.

KNOCK KNOCK

I'M ETHELBERT NEVIN AND I FORBID YOU TO DANCE TO MY MUSIC! IT'S SERIOUS MUSIC.

PLEASE COME SEE WHAT I'VE DONE WITH IT!

NEVIN WAS SO SMITTEN, HE SET UP A JOINT RECITAL TO INTRODUCE ISADORA TO NEW YORK SOCIETY.

LADIES HIRED HER TO PERFORM AT THEIR SALONS...

...AND AT THEIR SUMMER "COTTAGES" IN NEWPORT, RI.

DANCING FOR NY'S RICHEST, I BARELY BREAK EVEN. AMERICANS DON'T RESPECT ARTISTS. TO THEM WE'RE JUST UPPER SERVANTS.

WE MUST GO TO LONDON.

18

22

23

BUDAPEST 1902

27

SIGN HERE TO TOUR VIENNA AND ALL THE CITIES OF GERMANY.

WITH PLEASURE, MR. GROSZ!

NEVER AGAIN WILL I FORSAKE MY ART FOR LOVE.

GERMAN STUDENTS UNHITCHED HER HORSES.

DIVINE ISADORA! HOLY ISADORA!

BALLETOMANES REMAINED SKEPTICAL OF HER TECHNIQUE.

CAN MISS DUNCAN DANCE?

YOU MIGHT AS WELL ASK "CAN THE DANCING MAENAD DANCE?"

ISADORA REPLIED:

"THE BELOVED STATUE IN THE BERLIN MUSEUM HAS BEEN DANCING MUCH LONGER THAN I HAVE."

INVITED TO LECTURE AT THE BERLIN PRESS CLUB, ISADORA WROTE HER MANIFESTO.

WHY DO I DANCE WITH BARE FEET? THE HUMAN FOOT IS A TRIUMPH OF EVOLUTION. THE REAL SOURCE OF DANCE IS NATURE. THE MOVEMENTS OF THE OCEAN, THE BIRDS, AND SAVAGE MAN ARE NATURAL, BEAUTIFUL, AND ETERNAL.

BALLET IS STERILE BECAUSE IT IS UNNATURAL. UNDER THE SKIRTS, A DEFORMED SKELETON IS DANCING.

THE DANCE OF THE FUTURE

THE GREEKS EVOLVED THEIR ART FROM NATURE. THEREFORE, DANCING NAKED UPON THE EARTH, NATURALLY I FALL INTO GREEK POSITIONS. O IMMORTAL GODS, I FLING ASIDE MY SANDALS TO TOUCH YOUR LIFE-GIVING EARTH. I SING YOUR HYMN BEFORE THE BARBARIANS.

THE DANCER OF THE FUTURE WILL NOT REVIVE THE ANTIQUE DANCE, SHE WILL NOT DANCE AS A NYMPH, FAIRY, OR COQUETTE, BUT AS WOMAN IN HER PUREST EXPRESSION. BODY AND SOUL IN HARMONY, EMERGING FROM CENTURIES OF CIVILIZED FORGETFULNESS, NO LONGER AT WAR WITH SPIRITUALITY — THE HIGHEST INTELLIGENCE IN THE FREEST BODY.

IN Paris TICKET SALES WERE SLOW.

AT THE ÉCOLE DES BEAUX-ARTS:

FREE TICKETS FOR ART STUDENTS!

AT A PICNIC IN RODIN'S HONOR:

DANCE FOR US, ISADORA!

BUT I DIDN'T BRING MY TUNIC.

...AND DANCED IN HER CHEMISE.

SO SHE TOOK OFF HER DRESS...

ISADORA VALUED THE OPINIONS OF ARTISTS ABOVE ALL OTHERS AND ENCOURAGED THEM TO IMMORTALIZE HER.

RODIN CALLED HER:

SISTER OF THE BREEZES.

OUR SHIP WILL BE AS PRIMITIVE AS ODYSSEUS'S.

BOOM! BOOM! (STORM)

JUST LIKE THE "ODYSSEY"!

"HEAVED ON HIGH THE BILLOWING FLOOD... BURSTING IMPETUOUS, A SUDDEN GUST OF MINGLING WINDS..."*

* Homer

THEY KISSED THE GRECIAN SOIL.

THEY WALKED BEHIND THEIR MOTHER'S CARRIAGE.

NO ONE SLEPT THAT FIRST NIGHT IN ATHENS.

RAYMOND DISCOURSED ON PHILOSOPHY.

MORNING SILENCED THEM ALL WITH THEIR FIRST SIGHT OF THE ACROPOLIS.

32

THE CLAN DUNCAN IS SUFFICIENT UNTO ITSELF.

IT'S TRUE. OTHER PEOPLE ONLY LEAD US ASTRAY.

I MISS MY WIFE AND MY DAUGHTER.

poor Augustin.

send for them if you must.

ISADORA HELD A PRESS CONFERENCE AT HER HOTEL.

AFTER MY NEXT TOUR WE WILL MAKE ATHENS OUR PERMANENT HOME. FOR NOW I AM INHALING INSPIRATON AND COMPLETING MY EDUCATION.

MOST NIGHTS THEY LEFT THEIR HOTEL SUITE EMPTY,

TO CAMP OUT IN THE HILLS AROUND ATHENS.

RISING AT DAWN TO A SIMPLE BOWL OF GOAT'S MILK.

RAYMOND PHOTOGRAPHED ISADORA AT THE THEATER OF DIONYSUS,

DANCING FOR AN IMAGINED AUDIENCE OF THOUSANDS OF ANCIENT ATHENIANS.

LOOK, WE'RE ON A LEVEL WITH THE PARTHENON!

IT'S THE PERFECT SITE TO BUILD THE "TEMPLE DUNCAN."

IT WILL BE LIKE PLATO'S "REPUBLIC,"

WE'LL TEACH THE LOCALS THEIR LOST HERITAGE.

1904

GERMANY ADORED ISADORA

AND SHE RETURNED THE COMPLIMENT, CURLING UP EACH NIGHT WITH A GLASS OF MILK AND...

NIETZSCHE

KANT

HAECKEL

COME TO BAYREUTH AND DANCE THE BACCHANAL IN "TANNHÄUSER" AS MY FATHER WOULD HAVE WANTED IT.

SIEGFRIED WAGNER, SON OF THE COMPOSER, INVITED HER TO THE PRESTIGIOUS FESTIVAL.

IN HER OWN VILLA AT BAYREUTH, ISADORA ATTRACTED THE INTEREST OF FELLOW GUESTS.

That Grecian tunic barely covers her!

And you know, she entertains men while reclining!

BUT ALL MY AFFAIRS ARE CEREBRAL (after Romeo).

Slave of Aphrodite

BERLIN
1904

40

42

ISADORA DELIVERED A SHOCK TO THE IMPERIAL RUSSIAN BALLET FROM WHICH IT NEVER RECOVERED.

SERGE DIAGHILEY AND MICHEL FOKINE WOULD FOUND THE BALLETS RUSSES—

an orgy of modern exotica.

TOP BALLERINAS WELCOMED ISADORA TO THEIR PARTIES AND PERFORMANCES.

MATILDA KSHESINSKAYA, FORMER MISTRESS OF THE CZAR

ANNA PAVLOVA INVITED HER TO WATCH HER EXERCISE.

THIS USELESS TORTURE SEPARATES THE MIND AND BODY.

THERE'LL BE NONE OF THIS IN MY SCHOOL!

CRAIG WROTE HOME TO A FRIEND:

I'M NOT MAKING A PENNY, BUT I'M LIVING LIKE A DUKE.

WITHIN A MONTH, IMPERIAL TROOPS GUNNED DOWN PEACEFUL PROTESTERS BEARING ICONS AND PORTRAITS OF THE CZAR. "BLOODY SUNDAY" FORESHADOWED THE GLITTERING CAPITAL'S DOWNFALL.

BACK IN BERLIN, ISADORA AND CRAIG ONCE AGAIN FACED THE WRATH OF HER FAMILY...

...ALL OF WHOM LIVED ENTIRELY ON ISADORA'S INCOME.

AUGUSTIN (WITH HIS WIFE AND DAUGHTER) WORKED AS HER MANAGER.

HER MOTHER AND AN AUNT

ELIZABETH, WHO RAN THE SCHOOL.

THE ENTIRE SCHOOL, WHICH EMPLOYED COOKS, HOUSEKEEPERS, GOVERNESSES, AND PROFESSORS.

RAYMOND BILLED HER FOR THE BUILDING IN GREECE,

AND NOW HE ARRIVED WITH HIS PREGNANT GREEK WIFE.

ISADORA'S HOUSEHOLD STAFF AND MUSICIANS AND CONDUCTORS WHO TOURED WITH HER.

ADD ONE GORDON CRAIG (previously supported by his mother).

and all MY DESIGNS to REVOLUTIONIZE The Theater.

45

SNOWDROP IN THE DUNES

NOORDWIJK, HOLLAND, SUMMER 1906

WHEN HER
PREGNANCY
BECAME TOO
OBVIOUS,
ISADORA
RENTED AN
ISOLATED
COTTAGE.

Dearest —
Got a fine bunny house —
big dune on one side,
big dune on t'other.
Only I can see out.
I'm so glad to be
alone & think of you.
with you all is wonder
& loveliness — with
others, things
become common-
place.
your very
obedient
Topsy

CRAIG
CAME &
WENT.

MOSTLY
WENT.

Kathleen,*
Thank you
for coming!

The POOR THING!
SEDUCED BY
THAT MARRIED,
PENNILESS
CAD!

*A FRIEND FROM RODIN'S CIRCLE

47

49

POST PARTUM

I FEEL VERY NEAR THE MYSTERY— THE KNOWLEDGE OF LIFE.

WE HAVE NO MONEY! YOU MUST WORK AGAIN SOON!

SHE MAY NEVER DANCE AGAIN, CERTAINLY NOT FOR 8 WEEKS.
Dr. van Ness

THEY MET THE GREAT ITALIAN TRAGEDIENNE, ELEANORA DUSE.

WHAT'S SHE SAYING?

ISADORA'S TRANSLATIONS ERRED ON THE SIDE OF DIPLOMACY.

(That window is much too big!)

She loves it.

SHE WANTS YOU TO DESIGN HER NEW IBSEN PLAY IN FLORENCE.

KEEP HER OUT OF THE THEATER. I WON'T HAVE ANY DAMNED WOMEN INTERFERING WITH MY WORK.

CRAIG'S DREAMY BLUE-GREEN APPARITION WAS A FAR CRY FROM THE "OLD FASHIONED DRAWING ROOM" THAT IBSEN SPECIFIED.

?

ONLY Gordon Craig can save the MODERN THEATER!

THE STUNNED PUBLIC EVENTUALLY CONCURRED.

EIGHT YEARS AFTER SHE LEFT FOR EUROPE ON THE CATTLE BOAT, ISADORA WAS

BACK IN THE **USA**

AUGUST 1908

I'VE CREATED MY ART, A SCHOOL, A BABY.

BUT I'M NOT MUCH RICHER THAN I WAS THEN.

HOW CAN I DANCE IN THIS HEAT WAVE?

IN A BROADWAY THEATER, WITH A SMALL, INFERIOR ORCHESTRA:

AUDIENCES WERE SPARSE AND BAFFLED.

SERIOUS MUSIC FANS HAD FLED THE SWELTERING CITY.

GEORGE GREY BARNARD — I WATCH YOU EVERY NIGHT.

THE SCULPTOR? I'LL POSE FOR YOU.

55

ISADORA'S SOJOURN LEFT ITS MARK ON RADICAL AND PROGRESSIVE NEW YORKERS.

THIS IS WHAT A YOUNG, FREE AMERICA LOOKS LIKE!

Socialists

Unionists

Anarchists

THE "NEW WOMAN" ADMIRED HER FROM HER MORALS RIGHT DOWN TO HER SCANDALOUS SANDALS.

Votes for Women

ARTISTS OF THE "ASHCAN SCHOOL" EMBRACED HER.

SHE'S A fellow Rebel.

John Sloan

ABRAHAM WALKOWITZ MADE THOU-SANDS OF IMAGES OF HER DANCING. MANY WERE USED TO RESEARCH THIS BOOK.

60

NOT THEIR FINAL BREAKUP.

IN ISADORA'S NEW
DANCE TO GLUCK'S
OPERA,

ORPHEUS

IS ALLOWED TO DESCEND
TO THE UNDERWORLD
TO BRING BACK HIS
BELOVED EURYDICE.

IN "THE DANCE
OF THE FURIES,"
THE SOULS OF THE
DAMNED RAGE AT
ORPHEUS'S CHARMED
PASSAGE.

THE DRIVER WATCHED HELPLESSLY.

APRIL 19, 1913

DEIRDRE, PATRICK, AND THEIR NURSE ANNIE DROWNED.

67

69

70

WHEN ENGLAND JOINED
THE WAR, ISADORA AND
SINGER TOOK THE
STUDENTS — MANY
WERE GERMAN —
TO AMERICA.

73

NY

FALL 1914

ISADORA HUNG HER BLUE DRAPES IN A STUDIO AT 4TH AVE & 23RD STREET.

Utopia in a Steamer Trunk.

OLD FRIENDS GATHERED.

Mabel Dodge

George Grey Barnard

THE ISADORABLES DEBUTED AT CARNEGIE HALL, SANS ISADORA.

Echoes of an earlier Isadora.

79

ONE DAY A MONKEY BIT THE KING, WHO GOT AN INFECTION AND DIED.

WITH HIM DIED ISADORA'S HOPES FOR A STATE-SPONSORED SCHOOL.

THE DANCERS RETURNED TO FRANCE.

ANNA FELT COMPELLED TO LEAVE ISADORA AND THE GROUP FOREVER. WALTER RUMMEL ALSO LEFT ALONE.

AND IT WAS NEVER MORE THAN AN INNOCENT FLIRTATION.

SHE TAUGHT DUNCAN DANCE INTO THE 1970s.

PARIS IS TOO QUIET WITHOUT MY ARCHANGEL.

A TELEGRAM FROM MOSCOW: A NEW WORLD OF COMRADES — AND THEY WANT MY SCHOOL!

90

93

94

AT 4 A.M., THEY LEFT THE PARTY TOGETHER.

SERGEI ESENIN

26 YEARS OLD

PEASANT-POET OF THE REVOLUTION

ESENIN MOVED IN.

HUSBAND?

YES, BUT BAD ONE.

ADIEU, HUSBAND!

ADIEU!

HOW ADORABLE, JUST LIKE MY SON PATRICK.

@*#!!×@)?

HIS IMPASSIONED DEBAUCHERY SHOCKED EVERYONE BUT ISADORA.

LUNACHARSKY EXPLAINED THE NEW ECONOMIC POLICY.

SHOPS WOULD OPEN,

THEATERS CHARGE ADMISSION.

WE CAN'T PAY YOU, BUT YOU CAN TOUR TO RAISE MONEY.

NOT AGAIN! I CAME HERE TO ESCAPE COMMERCIALISM.

I'LL GO ON TOUR IF I HAVE TO, FOR THE SCHOOL,

BUT I'M TAKING SERGEI WITH ME!

WE HAVE NO EMBASSIES ABROAD. HE WON'T BE SAFE

UNLESS YOU MARRY HIM.

ON MAY 2nd, 1922, AT THE REGISTRY OF CIVIL STATISTICS, THEY BECAME MR. AND MRS. ESENIN-DUNCAN.

I'M STILL OPPOSED TO MARRIAGE, BUT THIS IS DIFFERENT, A SIMPLE FORMALITY.

IRMA FELT SHE WAS WITNESS TO A DISASTER.

HE'S SO NEUROTIC! BUT SHE WON'T LISTEN TO MY WARNINGS.

HONEYMOON ROADSHOW 1922

ISADORA AND ESENIN WERE THE FIRST COMMERCIAL PASSENGERS TO FLY FROM MOSCOW TO BERLIN. IRMA STAYED BEHIND TO RUN THE SCHOOL.

A FREE SPIRIT IN A FREE BODY

HEADLINES BLAZED:

RED DANCER SHOCKS BOSTON

SOME CLAIMED SHE WAVED HER WHOLE TUNIC, NOT A SCARF.

SHE WON'T GET A LICENSE TO PERFORM AS LONG AS I AM MAYOR OF BOSTON.

JAMES M. CURLEY

THE U.S. DEPARTMENTS OF STATE, JUSTICE, AND LABOR BEGAN TO INVESTIGATE THE ESENIN-DUNCANS.

PROVE SHE'S A SOVIET AGENT, AND WE CAN DEPORT THEM.

HER MANAGER:

NO MORE SPEECHES, OR THE TOUR IS DEAD!

ISADORA WAS UNREPENTANT.

WHY IS ONE PART OF MY BODY MORE EVIL THAN ANOTHER?

I STRIVE TO UNIFY BODY, MIND, AND SOUL IN THE WORSHIP OF BEAUTY.

"TO EXPOSE IS ART, TO CONCEAL IS VULGAR, LIKE YOUR HALF-CLAD CHORUS GIRLS.

I WANTED TO FREE BOSTON FROM ITS PURITAN CHAINS OF CONCEALED LUST."

SEPARATED FROM ESENIN, ISADORA CONCENTRATED ON TEACHING, CHOREOGRAPHING, AND RAISING MONEY.

RETURNING FROM A TOUR OF THE PROVINCES, ISADORA WAS GREETED BY 500 DANCING CHILDREN IN RED TUNICS.

LIKE A FIELD OF POPPIES! IN SPITE OF EVERY HARDSHIP, A NEW WORLD IS BEING BORN HERE.

IRMA AND HER STUDENTS HAD TAUGHT A STADIUM FULL OF CHILDREN.

THE DANCES WOULD BE PASSED ON IN RUSSIA, LONG AFTER ISADORA WAS GONE.

112

FRIENDS RENTED HER A SMALL STUDIO/THEATER ON THE PROMENADE.

IT'S PERFECT FOR LESSONS AND CONCERTS.

I'LL HAVE TO LOSE WEIGHT BEFORE I PERFORM.

HER 48 YEARS WERE SHOWING—AND THEN SOME.

SHE HAD SOIRÉES FOR THE CULTURATI OF NICE.

filmmakers
musicians
writers
picasso cocteau

IT'S A MIRACLE... BUT ALSO A TRAGEDY.

THE AMERICAN PRESS THAT HAD SNICKERED AT HER DANCING NOW HANKERED FOR GOSSIP.

ISADORA DUNCAN WASHED UP ON FRENCH SHORE

THEY WON'T PAY FOR MY ESSAYS ON THE ART OF THE DANCE — ONLY FOR A SPICY MEMOIR.

$

Big offer

114

116

121

After ISADORA

THOUSANDS OF MOURNERS
THRONGED TO ISADORA'S
CREMATION AT
PÈRE LACHAISE
CEMETERY
IN PARIS.

Isadora
DUNCAN
1877-1927

THERE WERE NO
RELIGIOUS RITES,
ONLY THE MUSIC
OF BEETHOVEN,
LISZT, AND BACH.

IRMA COULD NOT GET THERE ON TIME FROM MOSCOW.

BUT SHE DEVOTED THE NEXT TWO YEARS TO LEADING THE RUSSIAN STUDENTS ON

A TRIUMPHAL TOUR OF THE UNITED STATES.

IN THE SUMMER OF 1929 THE YOUNG DANCERS WERE INTIMIDATED BY AN UNOFFICIAL AGENT OF THEIR GOVERNMENT.

RETURN HOME NOW, OR YOUR FAMILIES WILL SUFFER THE CONSEQUENCES.

THEY RETURNED. IRMA DID NOT.

SHE HAD ALREADY BEEN DEMOTED FROM DIRECTOR TO INSTRUCTOR WHEN THE SOVIETS SEIZED CONTROL OF THE SCHOOL.

ISADORA'S INFLUENCE LINGERED ON IN THE SYSTEM, THOUGH THE INSTITUTION WAS RE-ORGANIZED AND EVENTUALLY CLOSED IN 1949.

IN EUROPE AND AMERICA, ISADORA'S DANCES WERE PASSED ON DIRECTLY FROM STUDENT TO STUDENT, PRESERVED IN LIVING BODIES.

MORE IMPORTANT, HER BAREFOOT LIBERTIES WERE TRANSFORMED THROUGH GENERATIONS OF MODERN DANCERS, FROM MARTHA GRAHAM TO MARK MORRIS, DOING THINGS SHE'D NEVER HAVE IMAGINED.

I WANTED TO MAKE YOU FREE, NOT TO MAKE YOU ISADORA.

BEYOND THE WORLD OF DANCE, HER LIFE, HER ART, AND HER MEMOIRS ENCHANTED MEN AND EMBOLDENED WOMEN.

SOME OF HER LIBERTIES WE TAKE FOR GRANTED, LIKE COMFORTABLE DRESS AND SERIAL MONOGAMY, BUT OTHERS, IN ART, ED- UCATION, AND MOTHERHOOD, ARE STILL EVERY BIT AS HARD TO PULL OFF.

BUT HER FREEDOM WOULD HAVE BEEN MERE INDULGENCE WITHOUT HER GRAND UTOPIAN VISION. WHAT SHE LIVED, SHE OFFERED TO THE WORLD, AND TO ITS POOREST CHILDREN FIRST.

$\int$ELECTED βIBLIOGRAPHY

Blair, Fredrika. *Isadora, Portrait of the Artist as a Woman.* New York: Quill / W. Morrow, 1986.

Duncan, Dorée, Carol Pratl, and Cynthia Splatt, eds. *Life into Art: Isadora Duncan and Her World.* New York: W. W. Norton, 1993.

Duncan, Irma. *Duncan Dancer.* 1966. Reprint. New York: Books for Libraries, 1980.

Duncan, Irma, and Allan Ross Macdougall. *Isadora Duncan's Russian Days and Her Last Years in France.* New York: Covici-Friede, 1929.

Duncan, Isadora. *My Life.* New York: Boni and Liveright, 1927.

Duncan, Isadora. *The Art of the Dance.* Edited by Sheldon Cheney. New York: Theatre Arts Books, 1928.

Duncan, Isadora. *Your Isadora: The Love Story of Isadora Duncan and Gordon Craig.* Edited by Francis Steegmuller. New York: Random House, 1974.

Kurth, Peter. *Isadora: A Sensational Life.* New York: Little, Brown, 2001.

Loewenthal, Lillian. *The Search for Isadora: The Legend and Legacy of Isadora Duncan.* Pennington, NJ: Princeton Book Co., 1993.

Roslavleva, Natalia Petrovna. *Prechistenka 20: The Isadora Duncan School in Moscow.* New York: M. Dekker, 1975.

Shneider, Ilia Ilich. *Isadora Duncan: The Russian Years.* Translated by David Magarshack. New York: Harcourt, Brace & World, 1969.

Acknowledgments

Thanks to all the previous chroniclers of Isadora Duncan's life, from her own charming and capricious memoir to the inspired sleuthing of Peter Kurth.

Thanks to all the artists and editors of *World War 3 Illustrated*, whose collaborative cauldron incubated my comics. Especially to Seth Tobocman, chief recruiter and instigator.

Thanks to Paul Buhle for his extravagant opinion and stubborn championing of my work.

To my editor, Thomas LeBien, for including me in his vision of nonfiction comics.

To Jezebel Jones and Percival Furbelow for making the job less lonely.